Usborne

Wipe-Clean
Phonics

Book 1

s a t p i n m d

Written by Mairi Mackinnon

Illustrated by Fred Blunt

Say the sound: ssssss
Write a big squiggly **S** in the air with your finger, and then on this page.

Use your pen to trace this **S**, starting from the dot at the top.

Draw a circle around the things that begin with **S**.

Write **S** next to the things that start with **S**.

Hungry frogs

Give each frog a long curly
tongue so it can catch a bug.

Start at the bug and
follow the curves
into the frog's mouth.

Yum!

You could draw more
bubbles in the pond, too.

Trace the **S** with your pen and write some more.

S S S ·

Sam the chef needs to hang up his saucepans.
Draw some more **S**-shaped hooks for him.

What is Sam making for supper? Is it sausages,
soup or sardines? Can you draw it in his pan?

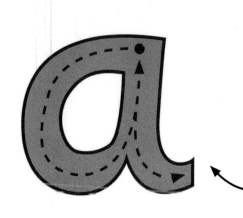

Say the sound: a-a-a-
Write a big round **a** in the air with your finger, and then on this page.

Use the pen to trace this **a**, starting at the dot and keeping the pen on the page.

Draw a circle around all the things that begin with **a**.

Meow!

Brrm, brrrm

Write **a** next to the things that start with **a**.

Apples and ants

Finish drawing around the apple shapes below.
Start from the dots just under the stalks.

Trace the **a** with your pen and write some more.

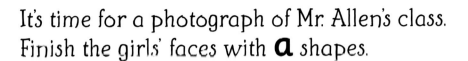

It's time for a photograph of Mr. Allen's class.
Finish the girls' faces with **a** shapes.

Mr. Allen

Akram   Adam   Alfie   Arthur   Ashwin

Amina   Alice   Anna

Can you think of any more
names beginning with **a**?

Say cheese!

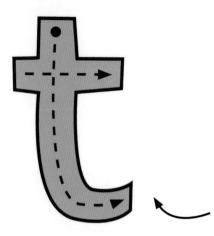

Say the sound: t-t-t-
Write a big, long **t** in the air with your finger, and then on this page.

Trace this **t**. Start at the dot and go down. Then take your pen off the page and go across from left to right.

Draw a circle around the things that begin with **t**.

Write **t** next to the things that start with **t**.

Teddy bears in the rain

Terrible weather today! Draw some handles so these teddy bears can hold up their umbrellas.

Pitter patter
pitter patter

You could draw some more raindrops, too.

Splash!

Trace the **t** with your pen and write some more.

t t t t

Finish the anchors with **t** shapes. Draw a circle around three more things that begin with **t**.

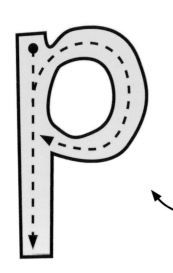

Say the sound: p-p-p-
Write a big **p** in the air with
your finger, then on this page.

Trace this **p**. Go down, then
up and around, keeping
your pen on the page.

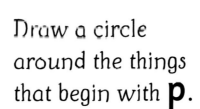

Arrrrr

Draw a circle
around the things
that begin with **p**.

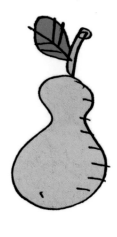

Write **p** next
to things that
start with **p**.

Penguins in the park

Look for these things and write **p** in the circle next to them:

- penguins paddling in the pool
- penguins playing ping-pong
- a peckish penguin eating pizza
- penguins having a picnic

Weeeeee!

Can you spot more things that start with **p**?

Trace the **p** with your pen and write some more.

p p p

Poppy and Patrick are in the parrot house.
Finish the pictures of parrots using **p** shapes.

Pretty Polly!

How many parrots are perching here?

Squawk!

Making words

Put **s - a - t** together and you get **sat**.

Read the letters.	Read the word.	Now write it.

s a t   sat   *sat*

What do you get if you put **p - a - t** together?

p a t   pat   *pat*

How about **t - a - p**?

t a p   tap   *tap*

Which picture is right for sat? Write **sat** under it.

1   2   3

Which picture is right for pat? Write **pat** under it.

4   5   6

....

Which of these is right for tap? Write **tap** under it.

7   8   9

....

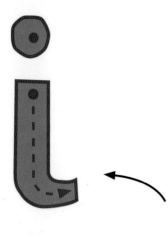

Say the sound: i-i-i-
Write a big **i** in the air with your
finger and then on this page.
Don't forget the dot!

Trace this **i** with your pen.
Start with the line, then add the dot.

Draw a circle
around the things
that begin with **i.**

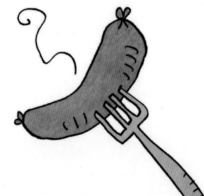

Write **i** next to
the things that
start with **i.**

Incredible insects

Each of these bugs should have six legs, but some of them don't.
Use the pen to add the missing legs.

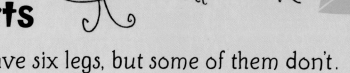

Bzzzzzzz

Bzzzzzzz

Trace the **i** with your pen and write some more. Start with each line, then add a dot.

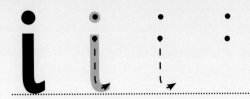

Isabelle and Imran both have their birthday today. Finish the candles on their birthday cakes using **i** shapes.

Say the sound: nnnnn
Write a big **n** in the air with
your finger, then on this page.

Trace this **n** with your pen,
keeping it on the page.

Moooo!

Draw a circle
around the things
that begin with **n.**

Write **n** next to
the things that
start with **n.**

Trace the **n** with your pen and write some more.

n n n

These nine fine elephants are out on parade.
Finish their heads with **n** shapes.

Hello!

Making words

Put **s – i – p** together and you get **sip**.

Read the letters.   Read the word.   Now write it.

s i p   sip   sip

What do you get if you put **t – i – p** together?

t i p   tip   tip

How about **p – i – n**?

p i n   pin   pin

Which picture is right for sip? Write **sip** under it.

1

2

3 Aaah!

Which of these is right for tip? Write **tip** under it.

4

5

6

....

Which picture is right for pin? Write **pin** under it.

7

8

9

....

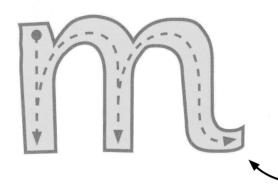

Say the sound: mmmm
Write a big **m** in the air with
your finger, then on this page.

Trace this **m** with the pen,
keeping it on the page.

Draw a circle
around the things
that begin with **m**.

Write **m** next
to the things that
start with **m**.

Munching mice

These mice need to grab some cheese and quickly scurry back to their hole.

Shhhh!

Mmmm!

Munch, munch

Draw around their ears so they can hear if Max the cat wakes up.

Trace the **m** with your pen and write some more.

m m m m

Molly, Minna and Marlon have gone swimming. Use your pen to finish their masks using **m** shapes.

Can you spot something else that begins with **m** swimming in the sea?

Say the sound: d-d-d-
Write a big **d** in the air with
your finger, then on this page.

Use the pen to trace this **d**. Start at the dot
and go around first, then up and down.

Ee-or!

Draw a circle
around the things
that begin with **d**.

Write **d** next to the things
that start with with **d**.

Weeeee!

Dinosaurs' day out

Look for all these things and write a little **d** in the circle next to them:

- a dinosaur diving into the deep blue sea
- dinosaurs having a delicious dinner
- two dinosaurs dancing
- a dinosaur dentist

Can you spot more things that begin with **d**?

Aaaah!

Hmmm

Trace the **d** with your pen and write some more.

d d d ·

Daisy, David and Daniel are feeding the ducks.
Can you finish the duck drawings using **d** shapes?

Making words

Put **m - a - t** together and you get **mat**.

Read the letters.   Read the word.   Now write it.

m a t   mat   mat

What do you get if you put **m - a - n** together?

m a n   man   man

How about **s - a - d**?

s a d   sad   sad

Which of these pictures is right for mat? Write **mat** under it.

1   2   3

....

Which of these is right for man? Write **man** under it.

4

5

6

....

Which picture is right for sad? Write **sad** under it.

7

8

9

....

Capital letters and small letters

You use capital letters at the beginning of a name or sentence.
Trace and then copy these letters. Start with the dotted line.

Ss

Aa

Tt

Pp

Ii

Nn

Mm

Dd